STONE AGE GEOMETRY
CIRCLES

Gerry Bailey & Felicia Law
Illustrated by
Mike Phillips

Crabtree Publishing Company
www.crabtreebooks.com
1-800-387-7650

Published in Canada
616 Welland Ave.
St. Catharines, ON
L2M 5V6

Published in the United States
PMB 59051, 350 Fifth Ave.
59th Floor,
New York, NY 10118

Published in **2014 by CRABTREE PUBLISHING COMPANY.** All rights reserved. No part of this publication may be reproduced, stored in a retrieval system, or transmitted in any form or by any means, electronic, mechanical, photocopy, recording or otherwise, without the prior written permission of the copyright owner.

Printed in Canada/032014/MA20140124

Authors: Gerry Bailey & Felicia Law
Illustrator: Mike Phillips
Editor: Crystal Sikkens
Proofreader: Anastasia Suen
End matter: Kylie Korneluk
**Production coordinator and
 Prepress technician:** Samara Parent
Print coordinator: Margaret Amy Salter

Copyright © 2012 BrambleKids Ltd.

Photographs:
Cover - Main image EcOasis (r) risteski goce Title Page – EcOasis (r) risteski goce Pg 2 – Gerald Lacz/age footstock/Superstock Pg 3 –David M. Schrader Pg 4 – MARGRIT HIRSCH Marco Cavina, Ryan M. Bolton, risteski goce eduard ionescu Pg 5 – (t) vedderman123 (b) mikeledray Pg 7 – (t) Caitlin Mirra (b) kevin bampton Pg 8 – Melanie DeFazio Pg 9 – From left to right RadlovskYaroslav, Oleg Golovnev, Lipsky, Gina Smith, George Bailey, Shutterstock, Jan Matoska, Karin Hildebrand Lau, Pg 10 – Heather A. Craig Pg 11 – (t) wildlywise (b) javarman Pg 13 – (t) Elena Larina (m) B. Melo (bl) shabaneiro (br) Tripplex Pg 15 – (l) Vladimir V. Georglieveskly (r) Luciano Mortula Pg 17 – (t) ruzanna (ml) CROM (mr) xpixel/ (b) Pavelk Pg 19 – (t) Henrik Lehnerer (m) Joanna Wnuk (b) Diane Garcia Pg 21 – (t) Marta P. (m) Tischenko Irina (b) Robert J. Beyers Pg 23 – Ian Bracegirdle Pg 25 – (t) Alex Balako (m) Selyutina Olga (bl) D&D Photos (br) alanf Pg 27 – (t) Jeanne Hatch (bl) Marcio Jose Bastos Silva (br) grynold Pg 28/29 – Scott A. Frangos Pg 29 – Oria Pg 31 – (t) Morozova (b) holbox
All images are Shutterstock.com unless otherwise stated

Library and Archives Canada Cataloguing in Publication

Bailey, Gerry, author
    Stone age geometry: Circles / Gerry Bailey, Felicia Law ; illustrator: Mike Phillips.

(Stone age geometry)
Includes index.
Issued in print and electronic formats.
ISBN 978-0-7787-0507-9 (bound).--ISBN 978-0-7787-0513-0 (pbk.).--ISBN 978-1-4271-8232-6 (html).--ISBN 978-1-4271-8238-8 (pdf)

    1. Circle--Juvenile literature. 2. Geometry--Juvenile literature.
I. Law, Felicia, author II. Phillips, Mike, 1961-, illustrator III. Title.

QA484.B35 2014   j516′.152   C2014-900418-4
                                            C2014-900419-2

Library of Congress Cataloging-in-Publication Data

Bailey, Gerry, 1945- author.
 Stone age geometry: Circles / Gerry Bailey & Felicia Law ; illustrated by Mike Phillips.
     pages cm. -- (Stone age geometry)
  Includes index.
 ISBN 978-0-7787-0507-9 (reinforced library binding : alk. paper) -- ISBN 978-0-7787-0513-0 (pbk. : alk. paper) -- ISBN 978-1-4271-8232-6 (electronic html) -- ISBN 978-1-4271-8238-8 (electronic pdf)
1. Circle--Juvenile literature. 2. Geometry--Juvenile literature. I. Law, Felicia, author. II. Phillips, Mike, 1961- illustrator. III. Title.

 QA484.B35 2015
 516′.154--dc23
                                            2014002244

LEO'S LESSONS:

MEET LEO

Meet Leo,
the brightest kid
on the block.

So that's Leo!

Bright as in IQ
off the scale,
inventive as in
Leonardo da Vinci
inventive, and
way, way ahead
of his time....

Block as in
Stone Age block.
Stone Age as in
30,000 years ago.

Then there's Pallas.
Leo's pet.

Pallas is wild and he's OK with
being called Stone Age, too; after
all, his ancestors have been around
for millions of years. And that's
more than you can say for Leo's!
You won't see many Pallas cats
around today, unless you happen to
be visiting the icy, cold wasteland of
Arctic Siberia (at the top of Russia).

THE TOOTH COLLECTION

Pallas has a problem. He often has a problem, but this one appears to be serious.
"OK, Pallas," says Leo. "What's your problem?"

Pallas holds out a large curved tooth. "I've lost this," he yowls. "It must have fallen out in the night."

"That's not your tooth," sighs Leo. "It's curved. Your teeth are straight. But open wide and I'll check."

"Not one missing," says Leo. "But this is quite a find. I'll put it in my tooth collection."

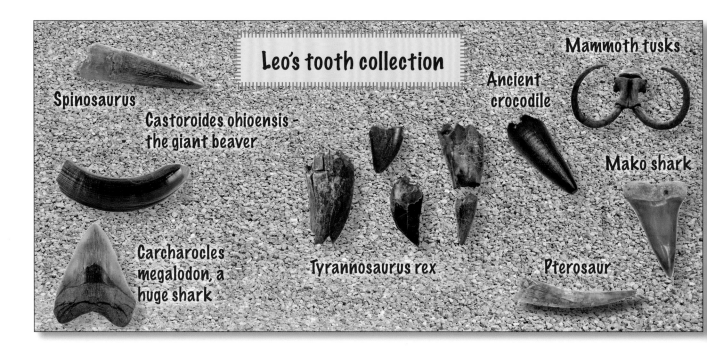

Leo's tooth collection

Spinosaurus

Castoroides ohioensis – the giant beaver

Carcharocles megalodon, a huge shark

Tyrannosaurus rex

Ancient crocodile

Mammoth tusks

Mako shark

Pterosaur

"These straight teeth belong to animals like you, Pallas, animals that grab things. They clamp down on things and hold them firm in their grip.

But these curved ones are for ripping. They hook into things and tear them open."

*This **extinct** kind of crocodile had straight, sharp teeth.*

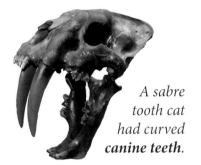

*A sabre tooth cat had curved **canine teeth**.*

"The mammoth's tusks are for fighting and digging in snow. They curve around so far, they almost make a circle.

Imagine having teeth like that!"

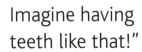

POINTS AND CURVES

You can show a point with a dot.   •

A point can be at the start and end of a line. A bunch of points lying next to each other forms a line.

•••••••••••••

If you have two points and draw a line between them you know where the line starts and stops. It forms a straight line from one point to another.

Sometimes a line isn't straight. The points that form it bend. This makes a curved line, or curve. A curve between two points is called an arc.

If the curve continues turning in the same way, it will finally come back to the point it started from. And when it does, you have a circle.

RINGS

"What's with the shovel, Leo?" asks Pallas.
"Are you digging?"
"WE are," says Leo. "We're both digging
and here's your shovel! There's a meeting of
the tribe tonight and they want a firepit."
"Easy!" Pallas says. "Dig a hole and light a fire!"

"It's not that simple. They always argue about who
is most important—who sits at the head. So we're
going to make sure NOBODY sits at the head,"
says Leo. "Good luck!" says Pallas.

Leo explains. "See this shape. It's a ring, or
circle. The fire goes in the center
of the circle. That way,
each person is the
same distance from
the flames.

Also, each
person is the
same distance
from the person
opposite them.

So as you see—no
place around the circle is more
important than any other place."

PARTS OF A CIRCLE

A circle is a curve that has
closed up. It has no end
points. Each point on the
line is the same distance
from the center.

The outer edge, or perimeter,
of the circle is called the
circumference.

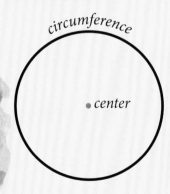

6

DRAWING A CIRCLE

You can draw a perfect circle with a compass or with a pencil, a piece of string, and a push pin.

Tie one end of a short length of string to a pencil.

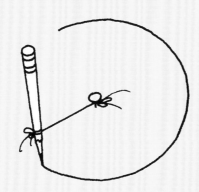

Push the pin into a stack of papers. Tie the other end of the string around the push pin.

Hold the papers as you slowly move the pencil around the pin, always keeping the string tight.

The distance across the circle passing through the center is called the diameter.

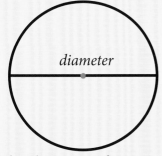

diameter

The distance of any point on the curve from the center is called the radius.

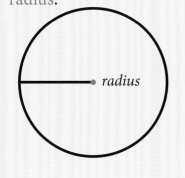

radius

A circular firepit used by Native Americans

A 14th century model of King Arthur's Round Table hangs in Winchester Cathedral, U.K.

King Arthur's Round Table

*King Arthur was a legendary British leader who was said to have lived in the 500s AD. He and his brave **knights** led the defense of Britain against invaders.*

Whenever the knights met, they sat at a round table. As its name suggests, it had no head, so everyone who sat at it was equal in importance.

7

SEEING CIRCLES

"It's a full moon tonight," says Leo. "Look, it's a full circle."

"It didn't look like that last time I looked," says Pallas. "There was just a thin slice up there."

"That's because it's moving around us here on Earth," says Leo. "And as it does, it catches the light of the Sun."

"But the Sun isn't there at night."

"It may not be there from down here," says Leo, "but the Moon can see it.

Depending on where the Moon is in its circle around Earth, the Sun can light up all of it—that's a full moon, or just half of it. It can light a bit of it—that's the thin slice you saw, or even three quarters of it."

"Or none at all," says Pallas. "And nobody can see anybody."

MOON SHAPES

We can see the Moon in the night sky because the Sun's light shines on it. As the Moon moves around Earth, more and more of it faces the Sun, so we see it as a quarter moon, a half moon, and finally a full moon. A new moon is completely dark.

new moon

quarter moon

half moon

full moon

Circles around

We see circles in action all around us. They're used as signs to give us information, as money, or in the shape of things we see in everyday life.

*Coins are usually **minted** in the shape of a circle.*

We use a circle to mark a special date on a calendar.

An instrument called a compass is used to draw a circle.

The Olympic symbol is in the shape of five interlocking circles.

A clockface shows 12 hours in a circle.

***Stonehenge** is made up of stone circles.*

People form circles to play games and to exercise.

9

HALF CIRCLES

"Wow, a cave!" says Leo, who is half way up the hillside. "Let's explore inside."

Pallas isn't sure. "There's some kind of animal living in there. I can smell it."

Leo isn't paying attention to Pallas. "It's the perfect home for a whiz mathematician. Just look at the shape for a start."

Leo points to the entrance which is the shape of a perfect semicircle.

"It's just that smell," worries Pallas. "It reminds me of..."

Leo still isn't listening. "I could make it cozy," he goes on, "by putting a door in the entrance. See—we just divide the semicircle into two halves. The two matching doors will swing open, and in we'll go."

Which is when Pallas recognizes the smell.

The bear smell!

SEMICIRCLE

A semicircle is actually a slice of a circle. It's exactly half of it.

A slice of a circle is called a sector.

sector

The base of a semicircle is the diameter of the whole circle. It's the line that passes through the exact center.

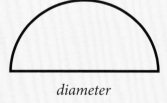

diameter

This peacock spreads its tail in almost a perfect semicircle. Its color and shape are used to show off to other peacocks.

This is the amphitheater at Epidaurus in Greece.

In the amphitheater

The ancient Greeks and Romans built outdoor amphitheaters to hold entertainments and stage plays. The amphitheater was a semicircle of seats surrounding a flat area called the orchestra that acted as a stage. Usually, amphitheaters were built on hillsides so the semicircles of stone seats formed a kind of **terrace**. Even soft sounds can be heard from the top rows of ancient amphitheaters.

11

PIE CHARTS

"Yeow, that looks good." Pallas's nose comes dangerously close to the steaming megaloceros pie Leo has been baking.
"Well it's not for us," Leo tells him, "so take your nose out. It's for the elders."

"And to stop any arguments," Leo adds, "I need to divide the pie so each elder gets EXACTLY the same sized slice. And that calls for a chart."

"The pie's going to get cold," warns Pallas. "Couldn't you leave the math until after it's been eaten?"

"No," says Leo. "We need a chart. Charts and graphs are useful because they map out information in a way that people—or cats like you—can understand easily. And in this case, we need to use a pie chart."

A PIE CHART

A pie chart can be used to show parts, known as sectors, of a whole circle. A pie chart begins as a circle. A slice, or sector, begins at the center of the circle and is held between two lines of radius.

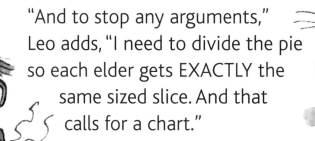

Each slice shows a part, usually called a fraction, written like this ¼, ½, ¾ of the whole.

Each part can also be written as a percentage like this, 20%, 50%, of the whole.

"Well, if it was up to me," says Pallas, "I'd just cut a big piece for me, and a big piece for you, and let them fight over the rest."

"Which is why they gave the job of dividing it to a mathematician like ME," says Leo, "and not to a greedy cat."

PIE CHART PIECES - TAKING THE BLUE PIECE

| One whole | Three quarters or 75% | Half or 50% | 1 third or 33% | 1 quarter or 25% | 1 fifth or 20% |

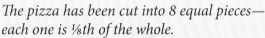

The pizza has been cut into 8 equal pieces—each one is ⅛th of the whole.

Your pie chart

Pie charts are used to record all kinds of information and data. You could make a pie chart of the different things you do in your day.

If your pie chart represents 24 hours, color in the correct-sized sectors to show how many of these hours you sleep, are in school, eat, play, watch TV, and do other things.

AROUND AND AROUND

The tribe is planning its annual sport day and Leo must come up with a new event. It's going to be an event that Pallas can join in, too.

"How about a cat show?" suggests Pallas.
"The most 'purrfect' cat wins."

"I think they mean a sporting event, not a cat sitting on a cushion," says Leo, thinking hard.

And then he gets it.

"Hey Pallas, I've an idea that's 'purrfect' for you. Come here, I need you to test this."
He holds up a circular band of wood. "It's a hoop. You put it around your waist and swing it around. The winner is the one who keeps it spinning for the longest time."

Leo's good. But Pallas has a hard time keeping the hoop spinning around his hips.

"Practice makes purrfect," says Leo.

CIRCLES SPIN

Circles move easily; they roll and spin.

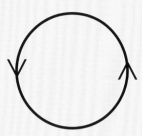

A circle can spin vertically. A wheel does this when it rolls along the ground.

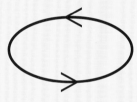

A circle can also spin horizontally, like Leo's wooden hoop.

The London Eye is a huge Ferris wheel that turns vertically very slowly.

A merry-go-round, like this one, is just a large wheel turned on its side. It spins horizontally.

15

WHEELS

"I don't think this is a good idea," groans Pallas. As he pulls a heavy sled on which lies a huge, dead giant beaver. "Can't you pull too?"

"I'm thinking," says Leo, "of a good idea that will help you." "And you can't think and pull at the same time?" asks Pallas. But Leo is already busy.

He slices 4 rings of wood from a large log. "So that's your brilliant idea," scoffs Pallas. "Wooden plates to eat the beaver off?"

"Wait!" says Leo. He drills a hole through the center of each disk. Then he places a pole through the hole and attaches it to the sled.
"Wheels," he says. "Not a bad day's work thinking that one up!"

Stone wheels were once used to grind grains of wheat into flour.

The wheel and axle

The wheel and axle is one of the six **simple machines** *used to do work. The wheel and axle is made up of a round wheel with a rod, called an axle, that sticks through its center. The center is called a hub. Usually the wheel and axle turn together. They turn around an imaginary line called an axis that runs through the center of the hub.*

Wheels at work

A wheel and axle can be used to draw water from a well. A rope with a bucket on the end is wound around an axle and the wheel is the handle that's used to raise or lower the bucket.

A turning wheel and axle is used to draw water from this well.

Wood has been cut and shaped into wheels for thousands of years.

RADIUS

The radius is the distance from the center of a circle to its outer edge, or circumference. Each spoke of a wheel is the length of the wheel's radius.

radius

center

SPINNING BLADES

"What on earth is that?" asks Pallas, pointing at the strange contraption Leo has built.
"It's my 'copter," says Leo. "It's a flying machine."
"You're never going to fly with that," mocks Pallas. "It won't lift a heavy thing like you off the ground."
"No," says Leo, "but it will lift YOU."

"No way!" says Pallas. "You don't even know it will fly."

"I promise you it will," says Leo. "It will fly like this maple tree seed flies. See these little wings? As the key spins around, it creates a force under the wings that lifts the seed and allows it to be carried along by the wind."

"So this is a giant maple seed machine with three wings," says Pallas, "and you want me to fly in it."

"Just strap the wings to your back, like this," says Leo. "Now climb the tree and jump."

"Just like that!" says Pallas.
"Just like that," agrees Leo.

An old windmill has a ring of spinning blades.

Nature's helicopter

The seed pod of the maple tree has two wings. It is known as a key. The key is the fruit of the tree. Both wings contain a seed. The key is shaped to spin as it falls from the tree. This helps the wind carry it further than other plant's seeds that simply drop to the ground.

A maple key

A helicopter in flight

Wings in a circle

A helicopter uses wings that move in a circle to lift it and hold it off the ground. The wings are called rotary wings. They are long and thin. Each is curved on top and flatter underneath. This means that air traveling over the top must move faster to get to the back than air moving underneath. The way the air moves over the blades at different speeds helps the helicopter to rise and allows it to fly.

19

WHEELS IN WHEELS

"Wow, what's that?" exclaims Pallas, looking at the machine Leo has built.

"It's an automatic cat-grooming machine," says Leo. "All I have to do is turn the handle that's attached to this big wheel up here."

"See the teeth in the wheel? They catch against the teeth in the next wheel and set it turning, too. And the teeth on that wheel turn the next wheel, which turns the next wheel..."

"That's brilliant!" says Pallas. "But which cat were you planning to groom?"

Leo tells Pallas where to stand. Then as the big wheel starts to turn slowly, the water pours, the shampoo froths, the scissors trim, the brush and comb smooth out the knots...

"There!" says Leo. "All done!"

CIRCLES THAT INTERLOCK

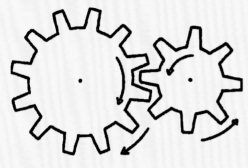

A wheel with teeth cut into its circumference is known as a gear. If the gear turns so that its teeth connect with those of another gear, it will make the second gear turn, too.

Any number of gears can be placed side by side and they will all be made to turn in this way.

These interlocking toy wheels will turn each other if one is set in motion.

A complicated set of gears helps turn the hands of this clock.

Gears in machines

Gears can be used to send power from one part of a machine to another. They can also be used to change the direction of the power. Using one gear that is larger than another gear can speed something up or slow it down.

Most bicycles have a set of three gears to help move the pedals at different speeds.

TANGENTS

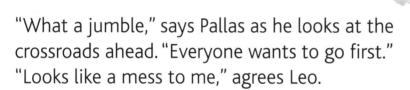

"What a jumble," says Pallas as he looks at the crossroads ahead. "Everyone wants to go first."
"Looks like a mess to me," agrees Leo.

"We'll have to do something," continues Leo, "this happens every week."

Leo scratches his head. "What goes in all directions at once?"
"Your brain," laughs Pallas.

"It's a circle," says Leo. "We need a circle with roads leading into it. The roads can cut into the circle at a tangent."

"A what?" asks Pallas.
"A tangent," explains Leo. "It's a line that skims along the edge of a circle. Like this."

Leo draws a circle with a line touching its edge. "Our new roundabout will have roads joining it at a tangent—instead of this jumble of a crossroads."

*Roads join this huge
roundabout at a tangent.*

Roundabouts

*Roundabouts are part of a road system.
They're used instead of crossroads.
Roundabouts allow traffic to move more
freely as vehicles don't always have to
stop, as they usually do at a crossroads.
Huge roundabouts on motorways often
have feeder roads joining at a tangent.*

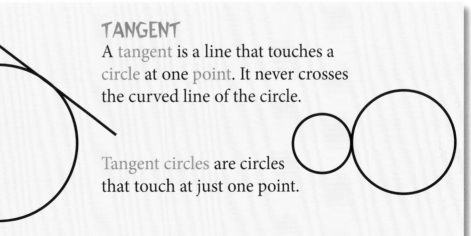

TANGENT

A tangent is a line that touches a
circle at one point. It never crosses
the curved line of the circle.

Tangent circles are circles
that touch at just one point.

CIRCLES INSIDE CIRCLES

"It's time to practice with our bows and arrows," says Leo. "We need a target board to shoot at. We have to try and hit it and we get lots of points if we're accurate."

"And what exactly does that mean?" asks Pallas.

"It means there are circles inside circles," explains Leo. "See, the board starts with a large circle around the outside and has smaller circles inside, until you get to the big dot in the middle. I'm going to call the dot a cat's eye."

"You can't," says Pallas, quivering, "it may be yellow like my eyes, but I don't want to be shot at by mistake."

"Just teasing," says Leo. "We'll call it a bull's eye."

CONCENTRIC CIRCLES

Concentric circles are circles that all have the same center. Each circle is the same distance apart from the one inside or outside of it, all the way around. The area between two concentric circles is called the annulus.

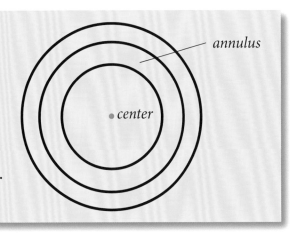

annulus

• center

Concentric circles in nature

You can create concentric circles if you throw a stone into a pond. The stone creates waves that branch out as bigger and bigger circles, one within the other.

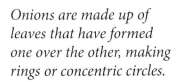

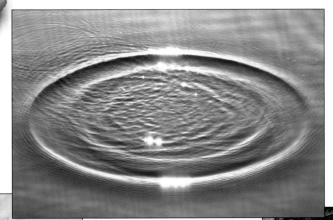

A stone thrown into still water will form concentric rings.

Trees grow by building up ring after ring of new wood.

Onions are made up of leaves that have formed one over the other, making rings or concentric circles.

Many flowers, such as this sunflower, form in concentric rings.

THE BOOMERANG

"A curved line will eventually come back to the point it started from," says Leo.

"Yeah," yawns Pallas. "You told me that yesterday."

"Just checking!" says Leo. "Because today, I want to show you something that does just that. It's my boomerang."

"I know this one," yowls Pallas. "You throw a stick and I have to chase after it and bring it back. And then you throw it again. And I bring it back, and you..."

A boomerang is shaped like a wing. If it's thrown a certain way, it returns to the person who threw it. Boomerangs like this are used for sport and fun.

"You're in luck! This stick comes back on its own. Watch..."

"So that was a circle?" asks Pallas.

"No," says Leo. "That was a huge arc that came back to where it started, just like a circle but stretched a bit. It's a special kind of oval called an ellipse."

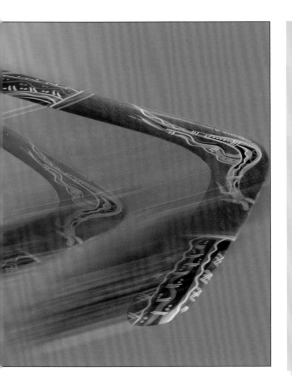

Ellipses around the Sun

*In the 17th century, the scientist Johannes Kepler discovered that the **orbits** along which the planets travel around the Sun are ellipses.*

The Sun lies at the center of all of these ellipses.

AN ELLIPSE

An ellipse is a shape like a circle that's been stretched in one direction. It looks like a squashed circle.

SPIRALS

"What's that you've built?" asks Pallas.
"It's a spiral slide," answers Leo.

"And ...?" Pallas goes on. "I mean—
is it one of your new mathematical
inventions?
Am I going to get a lesson on curvy
slides any minute now?"

"No! It's for fun," says Leo. "We're
going to climb to the top and slide
down, whizzing around and around
very fast all the way to the bottom."

"You know..." says Pallas, "sliding
and whizzing doesn't sound
much like a cat thing. Why
don't you go first?"

This famous spiral staircase is in the Vatican Museum in Rome, Italy.

A SPIRAL
A spiral is a curve that comes from a central point. It gets larger and larger as it twists around the point.

A conical spiral is shaped like a cone. It also gets larger and larger as it twists downward.

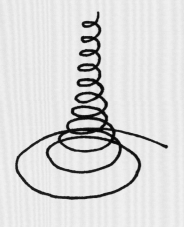

"But since you asked," says Leo, "the curvy slide is based on the shape of a curve that spins around and around, getting bigger and bigger. It's called a spiral.

"Some spirals just spin around like the shape of your lollipop. Some form a cone shape like my curvy slide."

NAUTILUS SHELL
The chambered nautilus has been around for hundreds of millions of years. It is made in the shape of a spiral. It has a series of chambers that move out from its center point. The nautilus grows a new chamber every four weeks and uses the old one to help keep afloat.

COILS AND LOOPS

"Look out," says Leo, pulling Pallas backward by his tail.
"Yeow," yells Pallas, "you nearly pulled off my tail."
"Well, you nearly stepped on that!" says Leo, pointing to the ground.

A large green snake lies coiled on the ground.
"Lucky for you it was asleep," whispers Leo.
"Let's leave it."
"Glad to," says Pallas, tiptoeing quietly away.

"I feel like coiling up and sleeping myself," says Pallas.
"YOU? COIL?" mocks Leo. "You can hardly bend over."

"Just you watch," says Pallas.

This amusement park ride uses loops to carry the passengers around and around.

COILS AND LOOPS

A coil is a kind of curve that looks like a group of circles or loops. Coils are used in many ways, from copper coils that help produce electricity to **raffia** coils used to make baskets or mats.
Coils can be wound one on top of another to make a kind of spring.

A loop is a curved shape that bends around and crosses over itself.

LEARNING MORE

OTHER BOOKS

Mummy Math: An Adventure in Geometry
by Cindy Neuschwander, illustrated by Bryan Langdo.
Square Fish (2009).

Basher Science: Algebra and Geometry
by Dan Green and Simon Basher
Kingfisher (2011).

WEBSITES

Get the facts on the circle and its properties at these entertaining websites:

www.coolmath.com/reference/circles-geometry.html

www.kidsmathgamesonline.com/facts/geometry/
  circles.html

Find a variety of games and activities with geometry themes.

www.kidsmathgamesonline.com/geometry.html

This website provides information on shapes and their properties.

www.mathsisfun.com/geometry/index.html

KEY WORDS

The parts of a circle.

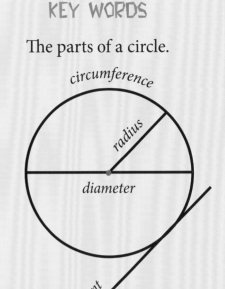

A circle is a curve that has closed up. It has no end points.

The radius of a circle is the distance from its center point to its edge.

The distance across the circle passing through the center is called the diameter.

The outer edge of the circle is called the circumference.

A tangent is a line that touches a circle at one point. It never crosses the curved line of the circle.

GLOSSARY

canine teeth Long, pointed teeth used for tearing food, such as meat

extinct No longer existing

knight A high-ranking soldier who fought in armor on horseback to serve a king

minted To make metal into coins

orbits The path taken by one object in space as it circles around another space object

raffia Fiber from a palm tree found in Madagascar and Africa that is used as a cord for weaving various articles and for tying

simple machines Machines that make work easier by transferring force from one point to another

Stonehenge An ancient monument in southern England made of tall stones standing in a circle

terrace A series of flattened ridges on a hillside

INDEX